9 Ways to Beat Social Anxiety and Shyness

How to Overcome The Fear So You Can Build Meaningful Relationships

by David Leads

This book is published by Relationship Up. Relationship Up publishes content on the relationships we have with ourselves and the relationships we have with others. Topics to help you be a better you. Check us out on the web!

www.relationshipup.com

Copyright © 2014 Relationship Up. All Rights Reserved. This book or any portion thereof may not be reproduced without the prior written permission of the publisher, except for the use of quotations in a book review. To contact the publisher please visit our website.

Legal Disclaimer

This book is presented to you for informational purposes only and is not a substitution for any professional advice. It is the reader's sole responsibility to seek professional advice before taking any action on their part. The contents herein are based on the views and opinions of the editor and publisher.

While every effort has been made to present accurate and up to date information within this book, the editor and publisher do not assume and hereby disclaim any liability to any party for any loss, damage, or disruption caused by errors or omissions, whether such errors or omissions result from negligence, accident, or any other cause.

The editor and publisher accept no responsibility for any consequential actions taken, whether monetary, legal, or otherwise, by any and all readers of the materials provided.

Table of Contents

Introduction

Chapter 1: Recognize What the Problem Really Is

Chapter 2: Try Exposure Therapy

Chapter 3: Find Your Passion and Get Involved

Chapter 4: Gain Social Experience through Social Media

Chapter 5: Leave the Past Behind

Chapter 6: Break Negative Associations

Chapter 7: Interact with the Assumption that Others See Your Value

Chapter 8: Ask Questions

Chapter 9: Shift Your Focus Away from Yourself

Conclusion

Introduction

Shyness has been a problem for people throughout history. Yet being shy does not mean you have to fade into the woodwork. Abraham Lincoln was an amazing communicator despite his profound shyness. Rosa Parks overcame her shyness and took a "stand" for racial equality. Johnny Carson changed the face of nighttime television even though he suffered from tremendous shyness, and Elton John became a megastar while battling the same issue. The shy Audrey Hepburn, too, became one of the world's most beloved actresses. Other currently popular stars, Johnny Depp, Lady GaGa, and Will Ferrell for example, go beyond their shyness to take their spots on the grand stage of life.

Why does all this matter? The answer is simple. Shyness or social anxiety does not have to define you. All the people mentioned above became successful in their own ways because they never let shyness stop them. If you feel awkward or anxious when you are in social situations, you don't have to sit back and live with it. You can make positive changes, show people who you are as a person, and have all the success you so deeply deserve. You can build better relationships, and you can enjoy them more fully.

Iconic actress Ingrid Bergman once said "I was the shyest human ever invented, but I had a lion inside me that wouldn't shut up!" Take your shyness or social anxiety as a challenge, and you can overcome it. Think of it as a problem you can solve, and you can claim your own power over it. Consider yourself a student of human interaction, and you can leave behind all your worries and fears about how you appear to others and what others think of you. You can connect with the lion inside you and become socially strong, just as Bergman and many, many others have done before you.

This book describes nine ways to overcome social anxiety and shyness. As you read, imagine how life will be different when you take charge of your daily interactions. Think about how your newfound social presence will affect your smallest and most significant moments. You can have the life and relationships you have always wanted to have. Believe in these possibilities and act with understanding and determination. Your socially well-adjusted future awaits!

Chapter 1: Recognize What the Problem Really Is

Children start asking the "Why?" question by the time they are about 3 years old. It just seems to be a natural part of being human to wonder about the causes for what happens in life. And if you are shy or socially anxious, chances are you have already given yourself a reason for it. But just as likely, you are putting the blame where it does not belong – on who you are as a person. Certainly some people are naturally shier than others. That doesn't mean that the shy ones are somehow defective. It simply means that they have something to learn that others already know. So the first step you need to make to overcome your social anxiety is to learn what it is and where it comes from. Here is a brief explanation.

How Are Shyness and Social Anxiety Defined?

Everyone knows what it means to be shy, right? The Oxford Dictionary defines shy as "Being reserved or having or showing nervousness or timidity in the company of other people." What some people get confused about is the difference between being introverted and being shy. If you are introverted, you prefer your own company and enjoy thinking and experiencing things in your own way, without much social interaction. Introverts can also be shy, but not all are. If you feel anxious or nervous when you are with other people, that is all about being shy and not about being introverted.

Social anxiety is defined by Thomas A. Richards, PhD, the director of the Social Anxiety Institute, as "the fear of interaction with other people that brings on self-conscious feelings of being negatively judged and evaluated, and as a result, leads to avoidance." In recent years, social anxiety has become a hot topic. The problem now seems more manageable to many people because they view it as a clinical diagnosis for which they can receive treatment. However, others hide behind the label and allow it to rule their lives. And there is no reason for that. No matter what you think about your shyness or social anxiety right now, if you want to be comfortable with other people, you can work to make changes.

Emotions Associated with Social Anxiety

Fear is the most common and all-encompassing feeling that shy people experience in social situations. Every interaction seems fraught with possibilities for failure and disgrace. Every word you speak might seem to have the potential of destroying your life or the lives of others. Therefore, you simply stop talking to others unless there is no other choice. The simple fact that the fear is irrational doesn't take away the desperate and upsetting feelings. But, at the same time, recognizing the fear as irrational can start you on the path to greater social ease. Here are some of the other feelings you can have due to social anxiety.

Inadequacy

If you struggle with social anxiety and shyness, you can feel very inadequate in social situations. This feeling can be especially strong when you see that someone you care about needs help but you are too shy to broach the subject. You might think to yourself, "If I was only better at talking to people, I could do or say something to ease their pain." The problem is that your social anxiety is the burden *you* have been carrying, and it has robbed you of the ability to do the good you would like to do. Begin to see it as something different from who you are, and you can learn to stop allowing it that impact.

Embarrassment

When you feel socially awkward and self-conscious, even being in the room with other people can make you feel embarrassed or humiliated. Thoughts about your social ineptitude, your struggle for words, or even the way you are dressed can circle in your mind and cause you to feel embarrassed.

What is worse, if you have ever been humiliated in a social situation, you might develop such a strong fear of embarrassment that you vow to never put yourself in that position again. When you carry this too far, you isolate yourself from those who could be your dearest friends. Don't worry. You can overcome the fear of embarrassment. All you have to do is learn to appreciate who you are and to expect the same appreciation from others.

Inferiority

Life is hard enough without going through it thinking that you are not as "good" as other people. Social anxiety can make you feel that others, because they are more outgoing and socially adept, are also more well balanced and even more intelligent than you are. This idea that shyness makes you less valuable as a person is nothing but a lie you have been taught to believe. If you question whether shyness has anything to do with inferiority, simply go back to the introduction of this book and think about the shy people mentioned. Did their shyness make them any less worthwhile? The most obvious answer is no. And neither does your shyness make you any less valuable as a human being.

Recognize the Problem in Everyday Social Situations

Researchers at UCLA took a look at how naming emotions affects the amygdala, a part of the brain that is excited when danger is near. Their conclusion was that when participants saw pictures of people expressing emotions, their amygdala did not sound the alarm if they named the feelings the person was displaying. So, when you are in everyday social situations, you can calm yourself by naming, either to yourself or to others, the emotions you have and that others seem to be displaying.

Once you are calm and rational, you can think logically about what is happening in the social situation. You can notice the real source of your social anxiety and recognize that the fear you feel is neither justified nor a part of who you are as a person. The next section can help you get in touch with your positive qualities and what makes you who you are.

Exercise: Who Are You and What Is Your Social Anxiety?

Get out three sheets of paper, a pen or pencil, and a thick black crayon or marker. Think back to a social situation in which you felt anxious, awkward or self-conscious. Write down everything you can remember about the experience. Include the setting, what each person said, the feelings you had during the interaction, how the conversation concluded and anything else that seemed important at the time.

On the second page, write "Who I am." Now, write nouns and adjectives that describe your positive qualities, characteristics and roles. Think about these words and how you can express these parts of yourself in daily social interactions.

Next, take out the third page and write about the source of your social anxiety. What about the situation reminded you of social interactions that turned out badly? Refrain from attributing the problem to your own perceived inadequacies or failures. Think logically and treat yourself as you would treat a friend who feels the way you did in this situation. This page might be difficult to write, especially if you have always blamed yourself for your shyness. With a little thought, though, you can see past your self-accusations and find the real reasons for your discomfort.

Finally, go back to your first page and your description of the awkward social situation. Pay special attention to the words you and others said during the interaction. Draw a circle around the things you said that did not express the you that you want to share. You have just marked the moments when your social anxiety got the best of you. Next, use your black crayon or marker to slash through anything in the conversation that did not express the positive attributes you listed on your second page.

Now, read back over the first page again, this time skipping the parts you have marked through. Notice the positive things you said and did. And if you find yourself dwelling on negative qualities you see in yourself, remind yourself that these are all just opportunities to improve. Only let yourself be defined by your positive qualities. As Oprah Winfrey once said, "I know for sure that what we dwell on is who we become."

Feelings When You Overcome Social Anxiety

Are you beginning to imagine what it might be like to leave social anxiety behind? If you imagine that you will never have another awkward moment again, try to look at the issue more realistically. You will likely still feel the occasional moment of uncomfortable silence or miscommunication. But here is the thing you need to remember: everyone does. Life will not be perfect once you learn to overcome your shyness and social anxiety, but it is decidedly better.

You can develop the same social ease as others around you enjoy. You can open up and express yourself without always feeling vulnerable to attack. You can listen to others without thinking constantly of how they are judging you. You can start feeling comfortable in your own skin.

When you overcome your shyness, you can start looking for reasons to spend time with others and stop avoiding social contact, because your generalized fear will be a thing of the past. And, you can feel better and stronger connections with the people you care most about as well as with others who share your world. By reading this book, you have taken the first steps on a path that will lead you to share your life and your true personality with those around you. If you stick to this road, you can arrive at your destination of social ease feeling safe, whole, and happy to be a valuable part of the human race.

Chapter 2: Try Exposure Therapy

Exposure therapy is a technique used by many mental health professionals to help people overcome fears. In fact, it is the primary psychotherapeutic treatment for social anxiety. A therapist who specializes in cognitive-behavioral psychotherapy can guide you and teach you coping skills as you gradually gain exposure to more social interactions. The process involves learning relaxation techniques, using cognitive restructuring to think about the situation in a new way, and putting yourself in social situations where you can practice healthy interactions.

Learn Relaxation Techniques

There are many relaxation techniques you can rely on when you have irrational fears like social anxiety. Some of the most helpful choices are deep breathing exercises, mindfulness, systematic muscle relaxation and visualization. When you employ these methods, you can focus your mind and emotions on the present moment and feel calmer as you face your fear of social situations.

Deep Breathing Exercises

You can relax anywhere by practicing deep breathing. Simply breathe slowly, in and out, filling and emptying your lungs each time. Notice the feeling of the air moving in and out of your lungs. With every inhale, imagine positivity coming in, and with every exhale imagine negativity and stress leaving your body.

Mindfulness

Mindfulness means being fully aware in every moment. You can do this as you practice deep breathing exercises or as you sit quietly. Notice the sounds, smells, tastes, physical sensations and sights of your environment. Release thoughts or worries about the past and focus on what is happening around you at this given moment.

Systematic Muscle Relaxation

If you feel muscular tension as you enter a social situation, you can relax systematically. Start with your right foot. Tighten the muscles of your foot as much as you can and hold them tight for about 10 seconds. Then, release the tension and let your foot relax. Move on to the left foot now, and then continue with every muscle group in your body from feet to head.

Visualization

Use the visualization technique to focus your imagination on a pleasant and comfortable place. You can choose to imagine any place that seems safe and happy to you. It could be a beach, a forest, a relaxing spot from your childhood or any setting that makes you feel more at ease. Close your eyes and picture the sights of this place. Imagine what you would hear, touch, smell and taste if you were in this place. Take a virtual walk around your quiet and restful place, imagining yourself interacting with this environment. When you feel calmer and more relaxed, open your eyes and join in the social interaction of the day.

Use Cognitive Restructuring

Cognitive restructuring, also called reframing, is a way to look at the social situation in a new, less threatening way. The first step is to notice the thoughts that are upsetting you. Therapists may talk these out with you or suggest that you write them down immediately after the social situation takes place. Next, identify the core beliefs behind the automatic thoughts. Finally, limit, refine and correct your response to the situation by either talking about it with a therapist or trusted friend or writing it down.

For example, you might find yourself in a situation in which your mind goes blank and you can think of nothing to say. You become more and more embarrassed. You might feel your face getting warm or your heart pounding harder. You might later realize that you were thinking "I am so embarrassed." Then, you might look at your core belief that is behind this automatic thought and realize that it is something like "I am a boring person."

Now, you can correct your response to the situation. That correction might go something like this: I am as interesting as most people. I might not be the most brilliant conversationalist I know, but I have done and said interesting things in the past. The other person also shared some responsibility for keeping the conversation going. I could have perhaps done better if I had listened more closely to the other person. But, I am learning, and next time will be better.

Practice Healthy Interactions in Social Situations

After you have learned relaxation techniques and worked with cognitive restructuring for awhile, start intentionally going into low-risk social situations. Before you enter these voluntary situations, do a run-through of how it might go. You can do this with a therapist or a close friend, write it down, or simply imagine how it might go. What might you talk about? How might you frame the interaction to look at it in a healthy and realistic way? How will you respond to comments about you or your chosen topics? And, if things don't go the way you expect them to go, what will you do next?

When you have imagined the interaction in a positive way, go ahead and put yourself in that social situation. Be mindful, paying close attention to your environment and to what the other person is saying and doing. Release negative thoughts and focus on the present. Make these first trial intentional interactions brief, since this will give you the greatest opportunity to have a successful interaction. As the character George Costanza says in an episode of the popular TV show Seinfeld, "End on a high note."

Notice That Nothing Disastrous Happens

After these first practice interactions, sit down and think and/or write about them. Write the consequences of what you said or did, always thinking realistically. Consider the impact of this one small interaction on your overall relationship. Think about the fact that each new interaction gives you another opportunity to improve your social skills. Finally, notice that nothing really terrible has happened. You have gotten through it. The successful conclusion of each short interaction builds on the next until you feel comfortable in these safest of social situations.

Increase the Social Risk Gradually

Start with an easy situation in which you feel safest and most at ease. Some examples might be a church group, a wedding or any social situation in which good behavior is expected of everyone. On the other hand, you might feel more comfortable in different situations. Choose whatever seems least stressful to you.

Gradually increase the amount of social risk you expose yourself to as you continue to practice interacting socially. You might start with a gathering of close friends and advance to a company function for your work, and finally, ease into the social situations that make you feel the most insecure and embarrassed. If you take it one small step at a time, you can eventually develop a stronger social presence and begin to enjoy being around other people more and more as time goes by.

Chapter 3: Find Your Passion and Get Involved

The most common cure celebrities have found for social anxiety and shyness it getting involved with something that they were passionate about and enjoyed doing. Following your heart can build your self-confidence and allow you to show who you really are. Your dreams of a brighter future can come true, but you need to actively pursue them. Whether you have only considered the activity you feel a passion for or you have dabbled in it enough to know that it makes you come alive just thinking about it, now is the time to make a commitment to explore it more completely. When you do, you can lessen your social anxiety and overcome your shyness as you become increasingly confident. The bonus for you is that confident people are more socially attractive. Not only can you feel better about yourself, but others can respond more positively to you.

Try a Sport

Many of the great sports heroes past and present have struggled with shyness and social anxiety. Yet, they all had to find a way to manage it and overcome if they wanted to have the success they desired. Magic

Johnson, Mohammed Ali and many others have dealt with shyness and come out on top. Why does this happen? The sport gives them an outlet for their passion and a way to turn that into social confidence. As tennis star Chris Evert explained her own transformation to a journalist, "I was very, very shy as a younger girl, just petrified of people. Tennis helped give me an identity and made me feel like somebody."

You do not have to be at the top of your sport to improve your social relationships, either. All you have to do is participate regularly and make it a significant part of your life. Choose a sport that displays your gifts, talents and skills in the best possible light.

Then, practice daily to improve your game. Work out with the others who follow your sport. Discuss upcoming sports events with your teammates. Think of a new strategy to help your team succeed and share it with them. If you are involved in an individual sport, look for opportunities to connect with others who engage in it. Conversation is always easier when you have something in common. And the great thing about sports for building social confidence is that, as you build your expertise in the game, you realize that you have something valuable to contribute.

Get Into the Arts

Acting

Theater Arts seems to be a popular occupation for people who suffer from shyness and social anxiety. If you think about it, it makes perfect sense. A writer gives them the words to say and a director guides them in their performance. The social pressure during the time they are on stage is significantly less for them than it would be in a personal conversation in which they might be lost for words or struggling to make a contribution to a conversation.

Another factor that makes acting so helpful for people with social anxiety is that it helps them feel a part of a group without the work of finding and gathering the friends themselves. Actor Michael C. Hall, famous for his role in the Showtime series Dexter, said, "I think I had a shyness about me, I think I discovered acting as a way to break out of that and as a way of belonging, a sense of being special." If you are looking for this type of ready-made social group to interact with, acting can do the same for you.

Music

Music can be a solitary activity, but it can also be a very social one. You can get together with others who share your passion for music for a jam session, for instance. Try collaborating with other musicians to write music. Your social insecurity fades as you work together to create the piece.

Many musicians find that performing gives them social connections that they do not make easily any other way. Marilyn Manson found this to be true and once explained "I'm kind of shy, and I think that I take that out by performing in front of a lot of people. That's how I get out of my shyness."

Writing

Writing might seem to be something you can only do alone, and for some writers, that is very true. If writing is your passion, look for ways to make connections with other writers. You can go to or do literary readings, attend or lead a writing seminar, or be a part of a writers group. You can also connect with your current and potential readers by having a book signing.

When you need to do research, try getting away from the computer a bit and talking to people who have experience with the topic you are writing about. For example, if you are writing a book about the Korean War, go where veterans of the war meet and have a long talk with them. This not only gives you background for and a better understanding of the subject of your book. It also gives you a chance to make friends and interact with people in a face-to-face conversation without the burden of struggling for a topic to discuss.

Visual Arts

If you don't know any visual artists personally, you might imagine the artist's life would be a lonely one. Yet many of the greatest artists of the past also had a rich and varied social life. You can meet other artists by going to showings at art museums. If you are just starting out, you can take art classes and talk to your classmates about art. When you are ready to sell your work, you can put it on display at an art fair and talk to the attendees who might purchase your artwork. Remember as you enter these social interactions that the key to minimizing your social anxiety is to focus on what others want to know about your art and be ready with the valuable information that can satisfy their curiosity.

Find the Right Career

Do you feel stuck in a job that does nothing to contribute to your happiness? If so, it might be time for a career makeover. Think of what interests you that you can do for a living. You have much more potential for success if you are passionate about what you do. And, just as important, you can build the self-confidence you need to enjoy more pleasant and less stressful relationships.

One way to look for a career you can enjoy is to read job descriptions for the kinds of work that naturally interests you. You can find job descriptions online or in newspapers. As you read, notice which types of job tasks are similar to hobbies or activities you like to do. Pay attention to how you feel as your read each part of the description. Eventually, you can find a career path that excites your passion and drives you to prepare yourself for the job of your dreams.

Volunteer

Volunteering is not just a way to help others, although it is that. It is something anyone can do. As Martin Luther King, Jr. said, "Everybody can be great. Because anybody can serve. You don't have to have a college degree to serve. You don't have to make your subject and your verb agree to serve... You don't have to know the second theory of thermodynamics in physics to serve. You only need a heart full of grace. A soul generated by love."

Tapping into this personal greatness within you, you can rely on the best parts of you to come out in a volunteer position that interests you. As you gain experience in the volunteer work you are engaged in, you can gain the confidence you need to connect with other volunteers as well as the people you are helping. You can connect more closely because you believe in what you are doing and have a passion for it. And, you can overcome your social anxiety and shyness because you know you are doing something valuable that others appreciate.

Chapter 4: Gain Social Experience through Social Media

How do you reduce your social anxiety and shyness by using social media? You can only do it if you approach it carefully and systematically. The reason is that social media has proven to be detrimental to social functioning when it is used haphazardly. Many studies show the harmful effects of misusing social media or using it as a substitute for face-to-face interactions.

One study showed that new social media users experienced greater levels of loneliness, depression and isolation from close friends and families. A follow-up study found that there were fewer of these problems for the same users a year later. A totally different study conducted at UCLA found there was no significant difference between users and nonusers in the amount of time spent with family and friends. And the social media users studied in the Pew Internet Project were even more likely than the nonusers to spend time at social functions and events as well as in frequent visits with local friends and family members.

So what is the answer? Is social media helpful or harmful? That might depend on how you approach it. If you come to social media with the idea of airing your innermost feelings, inappropriate or not, chances are the results will be negative. On the other hand, if you use it as a tool for change, you can have the opportunity to practice social skills and become more connected to the people that impact your life in a positive way. For ease of discussion, this chapter focuses on using Facebook. However, the same principles can be applied on other social media platforms.

Open a New Account

If you are already using social media, it is best to close that account and open a new account. Or, you can simply choose a different social media channel for your social skills practice. If you have never used social media before, set up an account on the social media platform you would like to use.

Be careful as you build your profile on the social media site. Only include information if you feel confident about it. For best security practices, it is usually best not to give personal information like your address, telephone number or birthday. A good rule of thumb is to only include information you feel comfortable sharing with a total stranger.

Choose Friends Wisely

When you set up an account with Facebook, the program presents you with several ways to add friends. You can tell it to search your email contacts for possible friends. For most people, this is not the best idea because you likely have people in your email contacts who you would not want to connect with socially. Also, Facebook might give you a list of suggested friends. Ignore this as well.

Facebook does not know what kinds of people you want to associate with. It identifies people who have factual information in their profiles that is similar to yours, such as people in the same city or who went to the same high school or college as you listed in your profile. After you have added some friends, it might suggest that you befriend people who are friends of your friends. Again, ignore this and choose each friend individually.

So, how do you decide which friend requests to make? The best way to approach this is to choose two types of friends. First, choose people you are close to and whom you come into contact with regularly. Second, choose people you know who make you feel good about yourself and generally have a positive outlook on life.

People will likely make friend requests of you as well. Use the same care and caution in deciding whether or not to confirm their friendship as you did when you made friend requests of others. You might also notice people making posts or liking your posts who you have neither requested nor confirmed. Sometimes Facebook allows people to add themselves as friends without waiting for your approval. If you do not know someone or do not want to interact with them, unfriend them or block them immediately.

After you have been on Facebook for awhile, reevaluate your friends list and unfriend or block people who have shown that they are generally negative, like to "rant" or do not treat you with respect. Be utterly ruthless in weeding out Facebook friends who do not contribute to your well-being.

Begin to Interact in Low-Risk Ways

Start connecting with others by liking posts you agree with. These interactions have a low risk of rejection because you are simply agreeing with something that has already been said. Like only positive posts that agree with your sense of what is right and good in the world, especially as you first begin to interact.

Next, you can start reposting pictures, videos or links that make your smile. Look for inspirational sayings and quotes that you can share. Repost funny sayings or jokes that are not likely to offend others. Be the positive influence that you would want others to be to you. If you approach Facebook in this way, you are likely to see many people responding positively to your posts by clicking the like button or making helpful or encouraging comments.

Start to Write Your Own Posts

Now that you have started interacting and seen that others generally respond well to positivity, start to write your own posts. Share something interesting that you have noticed while going about your day. Write posts that share pleasant family news like the addition of a family member through birth, adoption or marriage. Tell a silly story. Write about something you are proud of accomplishing.

Always be aware that Facebook interactions are somewhat unpredictable. Just as you might feel safer writing your thoughts and observations on social media, others might feel the same way. Eventually you are going to notice a comment or post that disagrees with what you said or makes you feel self-conscious or uncomfortable. When this happens, remind yourself that these are just words on a screen and cannot harm you unless you allow it. Then, counter negative words with positive ones, but do not let yourself get drawn into arguments.

Trust that these generally positive people you have so carefully chosen are basically good and mean you no harm. If you still feel that the comment was uncalled-for, disengage with the conversation and consider deleting that person from your friends list. Remember that ultimately, you are in control of who you interact with on social media.

Avoid Getting Carried Away with the Online Disinhibition Effect

In the journal of CyberPsychology & Behavior, John Suler, PhD describes what he calls the "online disinhibition effect." This is a phenomenon that experts have identified in social media interactions. It refers to the way people make posts and comments on social media that they would never make in a face-to-face interaction. This happens because of the anonymity, invisibility and time delay of internet interactions. It is the effect that prompts people to make posts that do not follow the normal restraints and boundaries present in the general culture.

Suler concludes that this phenomenon does not cause people to disclose their true selves, but instead encourages them to display a part of themselves that is not accurate based on their normal face-to-face interactions. And, this makes perfect sense when you are posting things that you would never want to say aloud to others.

However, it is this very disinhibition that can allow you to try new behaviors that you would like to incorporate into your new personal social presence. To be successful at reducing your social anxiety, you have to always have this higher self in mind as you make posts or comment on the posts of others.

Unfortunately, over-disclosure of negative feelings can lead to ending a valuable friendship, developing worse social habits or even losing a job. And, just as importantly, excessive displays of affection can lead to the very same problems. That is why you need to be careful as you are using social media as a way to change your social habits. If you do not make the right decisions most of the time, you can increase your embarrassment, self-consciousness and social anxiety even more. Therefore, you always need to be aware that you are less inhibited online and consider carefully the changes you want to make in your face-to-face social behaviors.

Present Your Most Grateful and Positive Self

Approach social media as a job you are working on to meet a personal goal rather than a free-for-all of every emotion that passes through your consciousness. Because people enjoy interacting with people who are grateful and positive, this is the type of persona you need to display if you want to have better social relationships with others. If a friend posts a picture you are happy to see, thank them. If they share a saying that makes you think, let them know you found it valuable. If they make a helpful comment, express your gratitude. You don't have to exaggerate the post's effect on you, but you can work on developing that higher self by showing you appreciate what others say and share.

Use What You Learn on Social Media in the Real World

Your work to improve social skills by using social media can never make your face-to-face interactions better unless you consciously apply it to the real world. After you have practiced on social media for awhile, look for opportunities to interact with family members and friends who are also Facebook friends.

Continue to project your most positive self image. Be just as assertive in choosing face-to-face interactions as you are on social media. Show your gratitude for caring and helpful words and gestures. When you feel comfortable in these social situations, transfer your new social skills to relationships outside this close circle. As you build social skills and increase your social contacts, you can begin to overcome your shyness and social anxiety.

Chapter 5: Leave the Past Behind

If your past seems to follow you around creating bad feelings, you are not alone. Not everyone has social anxiety, but nearly everyone has some bad memory that upsets them and changes the way they function in certain situations. The first thing you need to understand about these hurtful memories is that you just can't make yourself forget them – not instantly and perhaps not ever. But what you can do is deal with them in a systematic way, reframing them in light of what you now realize, forgiving yourself and others, and moving on to a more peaceful state of mind.

When you have social anxiety, it is natural to make excuses for yourself in social situations. You tell yourself that you would not feel this way now if something bad hadn't happened in your past. That may be true to a certain extent, but the deeper truth is that you choose to let these negative social experiences affect you. You do have a choice in the matter. And there is no time like the present to leave your past behind.

Reframe Your Past Social Problems

The first step to overcoming the past is reframing it in a new, more understanding way. This method was described in an earlier section as cognitive restructuring. Earlier in this book, the focus was on recent social interactions. Now use the same method to reframe incidents that happened in the distant past.

Maybe something unfortunate happened to you in a social situation in the past. You didn't stand up for yourself. Or, others were cruel to you. Maybe you were put into a situation in which you had no chance for social success. Examine these bad memories carefully to get at the bottom of what really happened. Give yourself credit for the good things you did in the situation. Acknowledge the weaknesses of others that contributed to your distress. Think about what you can learn from the interaction.

Put your negative feelings aside as you place the events surrounding them under the microscope of thought and reason. Did you actually make a social mistake? Or, did you say a perfectly acceptable thing that someone didn't understand or appreciate? Focus on the strengths you showed, even if your main strength was a childlike resilience that allowed you to keep on functioning despite the hurt. Can you do anything to change it now? You probably can't do anything about the distant past, but you can deal with it, learn from it and move on.

Forgive Others and Forgive Yourself for Past Social Blunders

When you feel unpleasant emotions like fear, resentment or anger regarding a social problem in the past, forgiving is easier said than done. What you need to consider now is that forgiving is not just a feeling. It is a decision you can make to ease your tension and social anxiety. Once you make that decision and act on it, the feeling of forgiveness can come much more easily.

Who in your past has made you feel undesirable, unlovable, unintelligent, worthless or small? Does the memory of what happened between you come up when you are in social situations? Or, is it a hidden, automatic thought that you no longer notice? Think of each person who hurt you and what it would mean to forgive them.

Remember that forgiving doesn't mean you accept their past behavior. It doesn't mean that you deny that you felt hurt in that moment. It only means that you no longer hold onto the resentment or fear. Release those bad feelings using stress reduction techniques. Let go of those awful memories and stop replaying them in your mind. Identify automatic thoughts that come as a result of those memories and replace them with positive thoughts.

While you are forgiving others, it is also important to forgive yourself. Again, it is usually those automatic thoughts that keep you tied up in self loathing and self blame. You might describe these thoughts as feelings, as in "I feel like I am bad with people," or "I feel like I am a poor conversationalist," or "I feel like I am not interesting." You might feel hurt, angry, sad or fearful because of these thoughts, but to forgive yourself, you have to realize that the feelings are based in thoughts. Then, make it a habit to negate these thoughts as quickly as you identify them as thoughts.

You may also have conscious thoughts about these past situations like "because of this, I can't function socially now." You can quit thinking this way by using a technique called "thought stopping." The next time one of these judgmental thoughts circles in your mind, say "stop." You can say it silently to yourself, or you can say it right out loud. Every time your mind goes back to that negative thought, use this technique until it goes away. The technique takes time to learn, but with practice you will find the negative thoughts going away without much effort.

Learn from the Past, But Then Let It Go

Do you often find yourself practicing conversations from the past that you wish you had handled better? Do you frequently go over what you would have liked to share and express? If you do, there is great hope for you. It means that you are thinking about how to improve yourself.

You are on the right track when you consider that a change is overdue. But, you need to start thinking of it differently. There is nothing wrong with considering how you might handle it next time, but think of it once and then move on. When the thoughts won't go away on their own, you need to consciously let them go. Instead of thinking about the past, clear your mind and relax. The other person is not likely to dwell on that situation. They have probably already moved on to other thoughts and activities. Allow yourself to do the same.

Focus on the Good and Happy Parts of Your Past

Just as nearly everyone has negative feelings from some part of their past, most people also have some happy times they can remember. Whenever you want to or can't avoid talking about the past, share memories that you feel positive about. Talk about the times you enjoyed in your past and how good you felt during those times. Nurturing this habit not only makes you feel more positive. It also gives you something pleasant to talk about when you are grasping for words to say during a conversation about the past.

Live Life in the Moment

Maybe the best way to put your past behind you is to live life in the present moment. Notice the sights, smells, sounds, tastes and physical sensations of the environment you are in during any given moment. Pay attention to what people are saying to you rather than what they might actually mean if you could read their minds. Notice their gestures in a nonjudgmental way and appreciate how they are able to express themselves.

Also, notice your thoughts as if they were sentences in a book. Are you going to keep reading this book, or are you going to put it down and look for a better book to immerse yourself in so you can take advantage of every moment of your life to its highest potential? Remove your past so far away that you are grounded in the now of the moment. When you do, you will have more mental and emotional energy to deal with the social situation at hand.

Chapter 6: Break Negative Associations

Shy people usually have some negative associations between events from the past and current happenings. After all, people tend to rely on what they have experienced in the past to guide them in the present. In many cases, relying on hard won experiences is helpful, but when you carry negative associations into harmless social situations you start out the conversation with a definite handicap. What you need to do to overcome your shyness is to find a way to break these negative thought connections.

Let Today's Circumstances Rule Today's Interactions

The fact is that prior negative consequences in social situations have nothing to do with the social interactions you are a part of today. In many cases, the people you had those distressing social experiences with are no longer a part of your life. And, even if you are in a conversation with the same person that hurt you in the past, you need to realize that today is a new chance to have a positive interaction.

Shy people tend to think that the other person in a relationship remembers all the hurtful things they said to you. They often believe that the person said those hurtful things from the depths of their souls. In most cases, these thoughts are just not true. You may be keeping score, but that doesn't mean the other person even remembers the words that upset you so much. They might have had a bad day themselves or said something without thinking much about it. You are jumping to unfortunate conclusions if you decide that you are going to always get the same reactions as you did in the past.

So, every time you go into a social situation, stay focused on today's interaction. Refuse to judge it from past negative experiences. If those experiences hurt you or caused you anxiety, they are not worth dwelling on and making a focal point of the current situation. Pay attention to what is happening now, in an open, nonjudgmental way.

Separate Emotions about Social Interactions from What Is Actually Happening

What do you feel when you come in contact with another person? Fear? Distrust? Vulnerability?

Insecurity? Inadequacy? Inferiority? Likely it is one of these if you are a person with social anxiety. The problem is that those feelings rarely describe or apply to what is actually happening.

Are you really afraid of this person? Perhaps you feel that way, but in reality, this emotion is probably not based on facts about the person. Look at the person rationally and know that they are human just as you are. Then, internally deny them the power to hurt you.

Do you actually distrust the person, or is the emotion coming from your social anxiety? You might feel vulnerable in social situations as a course of habit. But, remind yourself that you are only vulnerable if you accept the other person's version of who you are.

When you feel inadequate, remember the good things you have said and done. Give yourself a mental pat on the back for what you have accomplished in life and interactions you have handled well. See yourself as someone strong, and you will become stronger. When feelings of inferiority come to you, deny them any power over you.

The old saying "Sticks and stones will break my bones but words will never hurt me" is probably going a bit too far. Words can indeed hurt, as you well know. What you can reasonably say to yourself is a slightly less well-worn statement: No matter what you say or do to me, I am somebody. This saying acknowledges that people can say hurtful things, but those statements don't make you any less valuable as a person.

Exercise: Discarding Negative Thoughts

Negative thoughts lead unerringly to negative emotions. You might think that every thought that passes through your mind is based in the truth and is therefore valuable. However, thoughts are not something you are. They are something you have. And you can just as easily throw them away rather than hold onto them. Here's an exercise to help you do just that.

What You Need:

A small wastebasket
A stack of blank paper
A pen
Tape

What to Do:

Take a piece of paper and write a negative thought you are having. It can be a negative thought about a situation, about someone else, or about you. Take some time to expound on the thought, writing down related thoughts. Now, crumple up the paper as tightly as you can and aim for the trashcan. If you miss, get up and walk over to it and slam it directly into the wastebasket. Then, move on to another negative thought. Keep going until you have no more negative thoughts to write about.

Now, write something positive about yourself. You don't even have to feel that it's true. Look for something objectively good about yourself and write it on a paper in big, bold letters. Take tape and hang the saying on your bathroom mirror. Whenever you go to the sink to wash your hands or face, or brush your teeth or hair, stop for a moment and read the statement aloud. Think of this practice as a duty to yourself and a step towards more self-confidence. When you feel better about yourself, you will begin to fare better in social situations.

Chapter 7: Interact with the Assumption that Others See Your Value

Shyness and social anxiety can often be accompanied by feelings that others do not like you, do not want to talk to you, or do not find you a worthwhile person. But here's the thing to remember: It is you who are placing those judgments upon yourself. Even if the other person comes right out and says those things to you, it is you who chooses to believe them. Prepare for social interactions by taking stock of some of the values people bring into the social sphere.

Realize that People Usually Enjoy Interacting Socially

Some people like moments of solitude, and perhaps you do, too. At the same time, people are generally social creatures. They enjoy making new acquaintances and getting together to spend time with others. You might have the thought that you are not one of those "others" that people like to interact with. Chances are, this is not factual information.

Consider the idea that the people you come into contact with might be frustrated because you don't give them the opportunity to know you better. Think about how it would be to be the other person in the situation and imagine what they are thinking and feeling about your silence or awkwardness. As you do this, put the best possible spin on it. Assume that they are pleasant people who want to enjoy your company, because in most cases, they are. And remember: your thoughts have exactly the power that you give them in the moment.

Understand that People Generally Like to Make Friends

It's a fact that people generally like to make friends. They enjoy the feeling of being popular or well-liked. They want people to care about them and get to know them better. They enjoy the company of good friends. And guess what. You could be one of those friends and help them meet their need for social relationships.

Once again, clear your mind of negative thoughts and emotions. Let those upsetting thoughts drift gracefully down the stream and disappear around the bend of the river. Don't let your lying thoughts convince you that people don't want to be friends with you before you even give them a chance. Hang on to the thoughts you have that describe and affirm your basic goodness and your personal positive qualities. When you do, you will be in the right frame of mind to make friendships that can be stronger and more mutually beneficial than ever before.

See that People Like to Have a Good Time

People who have social anxiety commonly believe that others like making them feel bad. You might think that others enjoy hurting you. Or, you might think that you are not interesting enough to hold their attention or outgoing enough to be considered a part of the group.

In reality, most people just want to have a good time. Watch them when they are relaxed and sociable. Are they smiling? Are they friendlier? Chances are, they brighten up when everyone in the group is having fun. An old saying goes "Misery loves company." That may be true, but the opposite is also very true. People who are in a good mood like to be around others who are also feeling good and also conversing with them pleasantly.

You might not be able to *feel* happy in social situations when you are usually shy, but you can *act* happy. You don't have to flatter people excessively or agree with everything they say. You simply need to show them that you are as willing to have a good time as others are. It may seem harsh, but your social anxiety is not their concern. It might be on your mind constantly, and it might color everything you do when you are in social situations right now. But it does not define the social situation in the minds of others. They are usually more interested in enjoying themselves in the group than they are in excluding you.

Certain people seem to get a kick out of causing a disruption in the social process. They seem to thrive on discord and unhappiness. If you are shy, these people can cause you to feel panicky or even fearful. But here is what you need to remember: Although these negative individuals can be the loudest, they are not in the majority. The truth is that most people enjoy peaceable relationships. They feel uncomfortable with fighting and arguing. Most people, indeed maybe all people at the bottom of it, just want to be happy.

So, what can you do about this? How can you bypass the negative influence of troublemakers? You can remember that only you can decide how you will let them affect you. When others seem to back down and let the louder, ruder ones have their way, you can respond with positivity despite the negativity you are exposed to in the situation. You are in charge of who you become, not others. What you do, how you respond, and the decisions you make all go together to keep you as you are or to help you change into the you that you want most to be.

Notice that Others Have Needs and Desires to Express Themselves Just As You Do

As a person with social anxiety, you might feel that you have left far too many words unspoken. If so, you are not alone. It is a very natural inclination to want to express yourself. But here's what you might not be focusing on at all: others want to do it too. They want to say what they think and feel just as you do. They want to share their unique perspective on life and their own individual personality. They want to feel free to be who they are without fear of ridicule. Does this sound familiar to you? Most shy people would answer yes. And a part of getting over your social anxiety is understanding that, even if they do not feel the same anxiety that you do, the people you interact with still likely have the desire to say and show what matters most to them.

Yet you are not in a contest. In certain situations, you can definitely feel that way. It can seem like a tug of war where the win is determined by who gets to express themselves the most. Sometimes, shy people feel enormous stress during conversations where they want to say something and can't seem to squeeze in a single word. Then, often, when they find the courage to break out of their shell they overdo it by expressing too much. They don't give others a chance to say or do anything until they are finished having their say.

This over-expression usually ends badly. Others can get offended because you took over the conversation or feel that you are attacking them. It is much better to remember that others want to be expressive too. Get into the give-and-take of the social environment. Allow others to talk for awhile and then, just as importantly, give yourself permission to have your say as well. The free exchange of ideas can seem intimidating, but if you are going to become more socially comfortable, you need to start by saying a few things and then letting others speak. They will respect you more for this, and you can also respect yourself when it is all over.

Chapter 8: Ask Questions

Do you spend all your time in a social gathering trying to think of something to say? Social anxiety can cloud your thinking and make it hard for you to think on your feet. So generally, you find yourself saying nothing at all. Here's a new idea for you: Let others come up with what to say. All you have to do is ask questions and the ball is in their court. Here are some general categories of questions and how you can benefit from asking them.

Make Others Feel Good about Who They Are

You can show others that you find them valuable by asking them about the things they enjoy talking about. Ask the other person about something that really makes that person tick. Pay attention to what they are trying to express. Does that friend or acquaintance try to funny, intelligent or creative? Whatever they are trying to show is one of two things. Either it is something they already feel good about or it is something they want to feel better about. In either case, you can foster their good feelings about themselves. At the same time, they will tend to look more kindly on you and appreciate your company more.

What questions should you ask? Ask the funny one if she has heard any good jokes lately. Ask the smart one to help you understand a difficult intellectual problem. Ask the creative one what kind of art he enjoys most. Show interest in the things that person values most, and you will reinforce their good feelings about who they are and in turn, about your relationship.

Learn How Others Overcome Problems Similar to Your Own

Your social anxiety has been a problem for you. Perhaps it has been your most difficult problem. Others might not have the same problem, but they might have experienced something that was just as hard or required just as much courage to overcome. After all, everyone struggles with something, whether they show it or not.

If you see that someone has changed recently and become stronger as a person, ask them about it. Be the one to give them a chance to talk about how they succeeded in putting the problem behind them. Ask them if they have ever done something that was very hard to accomplish. Then, stop and listen. When they explain what they overcome, ask more questions about how they managed to do it. Ask how they felt when they saw the results of their effort.

You get several benefits from asking how someone overcame a difficult situation or personal challenge. You show that you see the progress they made, and in a subtle way, you congratulate them for it. At the same time, you build the relationship to a new level. You also might get some information that can be valuable to you as you meet your own challenges. And while you were doing all this, you are facing your own fear by engaging socially.

Find Out More about Others' Lives

People are interesting. They have interesting jobs. They have met fascinating people. They have done incredible things. Why not find out more about them? Most people enjoy sharing their lives with others, at least to a certain extent. When you are first getting to know someone, it is usually uncomfortable to get too personal. But you can ask the other person about the basic facts about their lives.

Ask where they're from and where they grew up. Ask what schools they went to when they were younger.

And, if they are still in school, ask them what they are studying. Find out where they work and what they do there. They are bound to have some interesting stories to tell you and experiences to share. As you listen, fill in any silence with other questions that come up during the course of the conversation.

If you begin to feel like you are doing an interview, stop for a moment and see if the other person will ask about you. They might not. They might be enjoying the attention so much that they are not focused on you. On the other hand, the fact that you asked those questions can make them feel more open to finding out the same things about you.

Talking to others about their lives enriches yours. It gives you something to new to think about and helps you understand people better. It might even give you the inspiration you need to live life more fully yourself. In the moment, it gives you something to talk about that the other person is interested in discussing.

Get Others' Unique Perspectives

Each person you meet has a unique perspective, just as you do. Any person's perspective begins with their genetic makeup, then their family life, their school, their culture, and finally, all the experiences and thoughts they have had in their life. That is why no two points of view are exactly alike. This can seem like a great hurdle to overcome, but if you allow yourself to value the diversity of human life, it can be a great joy.

So, ask people you meet what they think about current events. Ask them how they would solve a world problem if they had the power to do so. Ask them what they think of a book, movie or play. Ask them which sports team they favor.

Whatever you ask, ask with interest and with a real desire to see things in a new way. Then, listen. Don't stay concentrated so much on finding the questions to ask that you forget to pay attention to what the other person has to say. Be in the conversation. Be in the moment. Appreciate the other person's special point of view. And, don't forget to share your own in a friendly way.

Show You Care

Showing others that you care about them is a cornerstone to building close, lasting relationships.

Perhaps it is something you want to do, if only you could get over your social anxiety. But, if you wait for others to make the first move, you are going to give the impression that in fact you don't care about them at all.

So, it's time for courage. If you don't feel brave, that is okay. Acting with courageous intent will eventually give you the social strength you desire. When you want to ask someone how they feel or if they had a bad day, don't worry so much about how they are going to react. Instead, stay in the moment, ask, and then listen and watch to see how they do respond.

You might be surprised to learn that the other person has spent the whole day wanting to talk about what happened to them at work or in one of their activities. If they do want to talk, give them that opportunity. If it becomes clear that there is something you could offer them to help them feel better, go ahead and offer. Even if your social anxiety makes you doubt yourself, you can make valuable contributions to the lives of those around you. Come out of your internal life and reach out to others. More often than not, people are going to appreciate it and feel closer to you because of it.

Share In Others' Happiness

The best part of asking questions is that sometimes you get to share in someone else's triumphs. You get to enjoy their moments of happiness almost as if they were your own. And, you can be happy for them. There is nothing quite like being with a friend, a family member or even an acquaintance when they are excited and joyful. These are the moments to savor and enjoy.

But, what if you aren't there at the moment they get the good news or have the pleasant experience? In that case, their happiness might be a surprise to you. So, what you need to do if you want to celebrate with others is to get in the habit of asking them if they are having a good day. Pay attention to what you learn about them over the course of the social relationship and try to predict what might make them feel the happiest. Then, if you know this thing has happened, seize the moment and ask about it. Almost every time, you will be glad you did.

Chapter 9: Shift Your Focus Away from Yourself

Finally, this book would not be complete without addressing a habit of thinking that people with social anxiety suffer from the most. And that habit is always thinking about yourself rather than the other people in your life. British actress Penelope Keith put it very succinctly if a bit unsympathetically when she said, "Shyness is just egoism out of its depth."

Ms. Keith probably went too far with that statement. The fact that you are reading this book to learn how to overcome your social anxiety shows that you know you are not perfect. You know you have flaws just like everyone else, and you realize it is up to you to fix them. But there is an element of truth in what Keith says. Shy people do seem more focused on their own role in a social situation (and how they feel they are failing at it) and on how it affects them rather than on the content of the conversation or on enjoying what the other person has to offer.

Most likely, if you have social anxiety, you are having negative thoughts about yourself. But think about this: judging yourself harshly doesn't make you stronger. It doesn't make you smarter. It doesn't bring you any closer to the people you most want to connect with. It only makes you sadder and lonelier. So, start thinking about other people more. When you do, you will reap the rewards of better relationships within your social circle. Here are a few ways you can put this new, more sociable attitude you are working to develop into action.

Stop Dwelling on What Would Make You Feel Better

Feelings of social anxiety can be intense. That is perfectly understandable. Being kind to yourself is important, but it is also beneficial to let those feelings go. When the distress first hits you, you might not be able to ignore those feelings altogether. But eventually you are the one who decides whether to get stuck on the negative thoughts that foster those feelings or to move on to something else.

Instead of getting lost in your social anxiety, turn your mind towards others. Think more about what would make them feel better. Consider how you can make the conversation more pleasant for them without denying who you are. You don't have to let your social anxiety define you and take over your entire personality. You can interact with others on the basis of what you have to offer them rather than focusing on your own emotions.

Quit Trying to Read Others' Minds

Empathy is important in developing strong, healthy relationships. To empathize effectively, you need to imagine what the other person is feeling and what they need from you. But don't let your imagination rule your actions. Instead, take a guess at the other person's emotions and needs. Then, check with them to see if you are right.

You can make many false assumptions by trying to read others' minds without asking them if you guessed correctly. And, if your attitude towards yourself is generally negative, you are most likely going to interpret their words and gestures within that negative framework.

So, rather than trying so hard to figure out what others think without any input from them, stay with them in the conversation and in the present moment. Wait to see what will happen and what each of you will say. And remember, you are in charge of your own thoughts and feelings, not theirs. Give up on your desire to control the course of the social interaction. When you do, you can feel freer to enjoy the relationship for what it actually is.

Don't Think So Much about How You Appear to Others

When your shyness gets the better of you, you can get caught up in thoughts about how you appear to others. Shy people have reported becoming obsessed with their clothes, their facial features or the words they use to express themselves. Comparisons frequently follow these thoughts, causing you to feel self-conscious and disconnected. Giving in to these thoughts can only make your feel more uncomfortable in the situation.

You might wonder how you can stop thinking about something, especially when you feel anxious. You can't just banish those thoughts because when you try, they come on even stronger. However, there is a solution to this problem. It is simply a matter of refocusing your mind and filling it with other thoughts. Think instead about how others appear to you. Pay attention to the words and gestures they are using for self-expression, and notice that they sometimes say the wrong thing just as you fear you might. Concentrate your mind on what you like about what the other person is saying. Stay positive, let yourself relax, and enjoy the interaction.

Stop Waiting for Others to Show Interest in You

If you think that no one is interested in what you have to say, the problem might be something you have never considered before. It might just be that the other person took your shyness not as social discomfort but as a lack of interest or caring about them. Many people who have overcome shyness discover this when they start reaching out to others rather than waiting for others to connect with them.

You have to act bravely to take the first step. You don't have to feel courageous, just take steps toward letting the other person know that you find them interesting and valuable, and that you want to have a positive relationship with them. Acting on this desire, you can often make the friendships you want to make and decrease your social anxiety over time.

Start Thinking about How You Can Help Others

Pay attention to what the other person needs as you shift the focus away from yourself. Are they facing some major crisis that you can help them overcome? Or, are they generally dissatisfied with their daily life? How can you give them the support they need and inspire them to reach for a better life? Find out, offer help, and follow up with appropriate actions.

As you concentrate on being a helpful friend, you can begin to let go of your feelings that you can contribute nothing valuable to the relationship. You can reach out to others and appreciate their friendship more than ever before. The past will no longer hold you prisoner, because you will no longer allow that. And, given time, patience and practice, you can leave your social anxiety behind you.

Conclusion

Now that you have taken the time to read and think about ways to overcome your social anxiety, the next thing you need to do is make a decision. Will you let it rule and dominate your life? Or, will you face your shyness with courageous actions? The choice is completely up to you.

When you are ready to move forward, refer back to the exercises and information in this book. Draw inspiration from others who have faced and overcome shyness in their own lives. Reach out to the people in your social circle and begin to develop those relationships. Step out from the shadows and claim your right to express yourself just as others do. When you understand your power to change and act accordingly, you can become closer to friends and relatives than you ever thought possible. Best of all, you can finally feel peaceful in social situations and enjoy what others bring to your life.

Thank you for reading this book. We hope you found this information helpful and actionable.

Please write a review for this book and check out our other books on Amazon.

For more resources on relationships and to get in contact with us, please visit us on the web at http://www.relationshipup.com.

CPSIA information can be obtained
at www.ICGtesting.com
Printed in the USA
LVHW051755111220
673945LV00014B/1675

9 781502 766281